9/16

 W9-BYL-377

## DISASTER ZONE
# WILDFIRES

### by Vanessa Black

Alexander Mitchell Library
Aberdeen, SD 57401
3598415
DISCARDED

pogo

# Ideas for Parents and Teachers

Pogo Books let children practice reading informational text while introducing them to nonfiction features such as headings, labels, sidebars, maps, and diagrams, as well as a table of contents, glossary, and index.

Carefully leveled text with a strong photo match offers early fluent readers the support they need to succeed.

## Before Reading

- "Walk" through the book and point out the various nonfiction features. Ask the student what purpose each feature serves.
- Look at the glossary together. Read and discuss the words.

## Read the Book

- Have the child read the book independently.
- Invite him or her to list questions that arise from reading.

## After Reading

- Discuss the child's questions. Talk about how he or she might find answers to those questions.
- Prompt the child to think more. Ask: Have you ever experienced a wildfire? How did you stay safe?

Pogo Books are published by Jump!
5357 Penn Avenue South
Minneapolis, MN 55419
www.jumplibrary.com

Copyright © 2017 Jump!
International copyright reserved in all countries.
No part of this book may be reproduced in any form without written permission from the publisher.

Library of Congress Cataloging-in-Publication Data

Names: Black, Vanessa, author. | Black, Vanessa. Disaster zone.
Title: Wildfires: disaster zone / by Vanessa Black.
Description: Minneapolis, MN: Jump!, Inc. [2017]
Series: Disaster zone
Audience: Ages 7-10. | Includes bibliographical references and index.
Identifiers: LCCN 2016005782 (print)
LCCN 2016006338 (ebook)
ISBN 9781620314005 (hardcover: alk. paper)
ISBN 9781624964473 (ebook)
Subjects: LCSH: Wildfires–Juvenile literature.
Classification: LCC SD421.23 B53 2017 (print)
LCC SD421.23 (ebook) | DDC 363.34/9–dc23
LC record available at http://lccn.loc.gov/2016005782

Series Editor: Jenny Fretland VanVoorst
Series Designer: Anna Peterson
Photo Researcher: Anna Peterson

Photo Credits: All photos by Shutterstock except: Corbis, 6-7, Getty, 8-9, 10-11, 15, 20-21; iStock, 23; Thinkstock, 3, 19.

Printed in the United States of America at Corporate Graphics in North Mankato, Minnesota.

# TABLE OF CONTENTS

**CHAPTER 1**
It's a Wildfire!................................4

**CHAPTER 2**
Destructive Wildfires ...................... 14

**CHAPTER 3**
Staying Safe ........................... 18

**ACTIVITIES & TOOLS**
Try This!..................................22
Glossary .................................23
Index....................................24
To Learn More............................24

# CHAPTER 1

## IT'S A WILDFIRE!

Imagine it is a warm day, and you are walking home from school. You smell smoke. Your eyes dart to the far mountains. The trees are burning!

The wind picks up. Flames spread.
Soon the fire is blazing out of control.
It's a wildfire!

Firefighters arrive on the **scene**. They try to **contain** the fire. They do not want it to spread. Wildfires can do a lot of damage.

A tractor digs a trench. Firefighters clear trees and branches. They are making a **fireline**. They are trying to make sure the fire stops here. If a fire does not have fuel, it cannot burn.

## DID YOU KNOW?

Fires need three things: heat, oxygen, and fuel. Without these three things, a fire cannot burn. Increase any one of them, and a wildfire burns stronger and faster.

A helicopter comes.
It dumps water on the fire.
Another helicopter drops
**fire retardant** near the fire.
This coats the trees. It helps
keep them from burning.

The fire is not out yet.
But the firefighters
are happy. It seems
to be contained.

Wildfires are a part of nature. Sometimes they are good for a forest. They kill insects that harm trees. They clear away **diseased** trees. They make way for new trees to grow.

Other times, wildfires are destructive. When they blaze out of control, they destroy homes. They kill people and animals.

Some wildfires start naturally. They can start after months of dry, hot weather. They can also start when lightning strikes a tree.

In the United States, humans cause nine out of 10 wildfires. People are often careless with campfires and matches. All it takes is one spark to start a blazing wildfire.

# WHERE DO THEY HAPPEN?

In the United States, wildfires are most common in dry, wooded areas west of the Rocky Mountains.

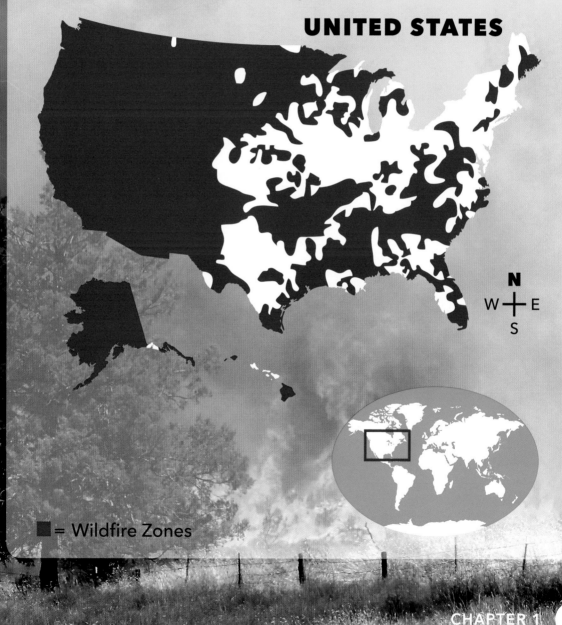

**UNITED STATES**

N
W — E
S

■ = Wildfire Zones

# CHAPTER 2

# DESTRUCTIVE WILDFIRES

Some wildfires are hard to contain. Even with firefighters on the job, they can still roar out of control.

Weather has a lot to do with how a wildfire burns. Wildfires love dry, hot, and windy weather.

In the Great Peshtigo Fire of 1871, 3.8 million acres (1.5 hectares) of Wisconsin wilderness burned. As many as 1,500 people died. The fire started from campfires. Some people tried to get away from the fire by going into rivers. The rivers became so hot, the water started to boil.

**DID YOU KNOW?**

Every year wildfires destroy millions of acres. They cause billions of dollars in damage.

# CHAPTER 3

# STAYING SAFE

Wildfires can start suddenly, without any warning. If you see smoke or fire, report it.

If a wildfire is near your home, listen to the **authorities**. If they tell you to **evacuate**, get out.

smoke detector

You can help **prevent** wildfires. Do not play with matches or fire. Make sure all campfires are completely out. Dump water on hot coals. If you see something that looks like a fire **hazard**, let an adult know.

Be fire safe! Make sure you have **smoke detectors** in your home. Check them once a month.

Be prepared, and you can stay safe in a wildfire.

# ACTIVITIES & TOOLS

## TRY THIS!

### EXPLORE A WILDFIRE

In this activity, you will use the Internet to learn more about a wildfire. If you need help using the Internet, ask an adult.

Find out if there has been a wildfire in your area. If not, has there been an especially significant wildfire in recent memory? You may decide to learn more about the wildfire you read about in this book. Learn everything you can about your wildfire. Answer the following questions:

① Where and when did the wildfire occur?

② What caused the wildfire?

③ How long did it take to contain? What resources were used?

④ How much area did it burn?

⑤ Did it destroy any developed areas? What was the cost of the damages?

⑥ Is there anything special or unusual about the wildfire?

# GLOSSARY

**authorities:** People in charge.

**contain:** Keep under control.

**diseased:** Having a bad sickness.

**evacuate:** To leave a place because of danger.

**fireline:** A place where people remove all fuel for a fire in order to stop the fire's spread.

**fire retardant:** A substance put on things that makes them not burn as easily.

**hazard:** Something that is dangerous.

**prevent:** To keep from happening.

**scene:** The place something is happening.

**smoke detector:** An alarm that activates automatically when it detects smoke.

campfires 12, 16, 21

causes 12

containment 6, 9, 14

damage 6, 10, 16

deaths 10, 16

evacuation 19

firefighters 6, 9, 14

fireline 6

fire retardant 9

fuel 6

Great Peshtigo Fire 16

heat 6, 12, 15

helicopter 9

insects 10

lightning 12

mountains 4, 13

oxygen 6

prevention 21

smoke 4, 18

smoke detectors 21

trees 4, 6, 9, 10, 12

trench 6

weather 15

wind 5, 15

# TO LEARN MORE

Learning more is as easy as 1, 2, 3.

1) Go to www.factsurfer.com

2) Enter "wildfires" into the search box.

3) Click the "Surf" button to see a list of websites.

With factsurfer, finding more information is just a click away.